OBAMA
ON ENERGY
INDEPENDENCE

M.T. BOOKS
PUBLISHER

ISBN-10: 1461035465
EAN-13: 9781461035466

OBAMA
ON ENERGY
INDEPENDENCE

A.CORN

ABOUT THE AUTHOR

The author **A. Corn** is a mysterious writer with no other literary works to speak of. There is no information about where A. Corn came from. It appears that A. Corn is simply a book organizer.

What we can say about the author is that he or she produced a body of work that accurately depicts how Obama defines his platform on achieving energy independence in the United States.

We believe the author really dug into the research that was required to produce such a fine piece of writing.

It is our estimate that A. Corn took several years to compile the data needed to complete this book. Rumor has it that if this first A. Corn book does well enough, there are additional works waiting in the wings.

The American public is hungry for the truth, and will most likely embrace the next A. Corn literary masterpiece.

Dedication

This book is dedicated to all of the companies, entrepreneurs, risk takers, and rugged individuals who really do care about our energy independence. We appreciate your efforts to put it on the line each and every day to make sure our great nation is able to power up and move forward.

Thank you!

TABLE OF CONTENTS

BACKWARD

It is traditional to read a FORWARD at the beginning of a book. Not this time, and not this book.

This book, 'Obama on Energy Independence' represents a reversal as to how our country is being led with respect to our current and future energy needs.

The word 'BACKWARD' provides the reader with a much better description as to the policies and beliefs of Obama.

Although this book portrays Obama in a satirical fashion, there is nothing humorous about how he is setting the United States up for failure when it comes to achieving our own energy independence.

Let us not forget who this book is dedicated to... **the people who operate our oil companies, our coal companies, and our utility companies.** These individuals and organizations constantly risk their lives and money to make sure that when we pull up to a gas pump, it flows... when we flip a switch, it turns on... and when we transport our goods, they get there.

The FREE market is the system we support. The FREE market is a proven winner. The FREE market has to be defended by the people who value it the most.

The Obama track record does not respect, believe-in, or value our free market. Living a life in academia prohibits an individual from experiencing the American Way. Obama has no experience with operating a business, risking capital, meeting a payroll, or creating REAL jobs.

We hope you enjoy this book, or what there is of it, because sometimes a lot can be said in very few words.

CHAPTER I

MY EXPERIENCE IN THE OIL INDUSTRY

CONTENT NOT AVAILABLE

(PAGE INTENTIONALLY LEFT BLANK.)

CONTENT NOT AVAILABLE

☹

(PAGE INTENTIONALLY LEFT BLANK.)

CONTENT NOT AVAILABLE

☹

(PAGE INTENTIONALLY LEFT BLANK.)

CONTENT NOT AVAILABLE

☹

(PAGE INTENTIONALLY LEFT BLANK.)

CONTENT NOT AVAILABLE

☹

(PAGE INTENTIONALLY LEFT BLANK.)

CONTENT NOT AVAILABLE

(PAGE INTENTIONALLY LEFT BLANK.)

CONTENT NOT AVAILABLE

(PAGE INTENTIONALLY LEFT BLANK.)

CONTENT NOT AVAILABLE

☹

(PAGE INTENTIONALLY LEFT BLANK.)

CONTENT NOT AVAILABLE

(PAGE INTENTIONALLY LEFT BLANK.)

CONTENT NOT AVAILABLE

☹

(PAGE INTENTIONALLY LEFT BLANK.)

CONTENT NOT AVAILABLE

☹

(PAGE INTENTIONALLY LEFT BLANK.)

CHAPTER II

THE BENEFITS OF $5 PER GALLON GAS

CONTENT NOT AVAILABLE

(PAGE INTENTIONALLY LEFT BLANK.)

CONTENT NOT AVAILABLE

☹

(PAGE INTENTIONALLY LEFT BLANK.)

CONTENT NOT AVAILABLE

☹

(PAGE INTENTIONALLY LEFT BLANK.)

CONTENT NOT AVAILABLE

CONTENT NOT AVAILABLE

(PAGE INTENTIONALLY LEFT BLANK.)

CONTENT NOT AVAILABLE

☹

(PAGE INTENTIONALLY LEFT BLANK.)

CONTENT NOT AVAILABLE

(PAGE INTENTIONALLY LEFT BLANK.)

CONTENT NOT AVAILABLE

☹

(PAGE INTENTIONALLY LEFT BLANK.)

CONTENT NOT AVAILABLE

☹

(PAGE INTENTIONALLY LEFT BLANK.)

CONTENT NOT AVAILABLE

☹

(PAGE INTENTIONALLY LEFT BLANK.)

CONTENT NOT AVAILABLE

(PAGE INTENTIONALLY LEFT BLANK.)

CHAPTER III

THE GREAT WORKS OF OUR 17,000 EPA EMPLOYEES

CONTENT NOT AVAILABLE

(PAGE INTENTIONALLY LEFT BLANK.)

CONTENT NOT AVAILABLE

☹

(PAGE INTENTIONALLY LEFT BLANK.)

CONTENT NOT AVAILABLE

(PAGE INTENTIONALLY LEFT BLANK.)

CONTENT NOT AVAILABLE

☹

(PAGE INTENTIONALLY LEFT BLANK.)

CONTENT NOT AVAILABLE

(PAGE INTENTIONALLY LEFT BLANK.)

CONTENT NOT AVAILABLE

☹

(PAGE INTENTIONALLY LEFT BLANK.)

CONTENT NOT AVAILABLE

☹

(PAGE INTENTIONALLY LEFT BLANK.)

CONTENT NOT AVAILABLE

☹

(PAGE INTENTIONALLY LEFT BLANK.)

CONTENT NOT AVAILABLE

☹

(PAGE INTENTIONALLY LEFT BLANK.)

CONTENT NOT AVAILABLE

☹

(PAGE INTENTIONALLY LEFT BLANK.)

CONTENT NOT AVAILABLE

(PAGE INTENTIONALLY LEFT BLANK.)

CHAPTER IV

HOW TO FIND COMMON GROUND
WITH REPUBLICANS.

CONTENT NOT AVAILABLE

(PAGE INTENTIONALLY LEFT BLANK.)

CONTENT NOT AVAILABLE

☹

(PAGE INTENTIONALLY LEFT BLANK.)

CONTENT NOT AVAILABLE

(PAGE INTENTIONALLY LEFT BLANK.)

CONTENT NOT AVAILABLE

☹

(PAGE INTENTIONALLY LEFT BLANK.)

CONTENT NOT AVAILABLE

☹

(PAGE INTENTIONALLY LEFT BLANK.)

CONTENT NOT AVAILABLE

(PAGE INTENTIONALLY LEFT BLANK.)

CONTENT NOT AVAILABLE

(PAGE INTENTIONALLY LEFT BLANK.)

CONTENT NOT AVAILABLE

☹

(PAGE INTENTIONALLY LEFT BLANK.)

CONTENT NOT AVAILABLE

(PAGE INTENTIONALLY LEFT BLANK.)

CONTENT NOT AVAILABLE

☹

(PAGE INTENTIONALLY LEFT BLANK.)

CONTENT NOT AVAILABLE

(PAGE INTENTIONALLY LEFT BLANK.)

CHAPTER V

WHY DEEP WATER DRILLING IS BAD FOR AMERICA

CONTENT NOT AVAILABLE

☹

(PAGE INTENTIONALLY LEFT BLANK.)

CONTENT NOT AVAILABLE

(PAGE INTENTIONALLY LEFT BLANK.)

CONTENT NOT AVAILABLE

(PAGE INTENTIONALLY LEFT BLANK.)

CONTENT NOT AVAILABLE

(PAGE INTENTIONALLY LEFT BLANK.)

CONTENT NOT AVAILABLE

(PAGE INTENTIONALLY LEFT BLANK.)

CONTENT NOT AVAILABLE

(PAGE INTENTIONALLY LEFT BLANK.)

CONTENT NOT AVAILABLE

(PAGE INTENTIONALLY LEFT BLANK.)

CONTENT NOT AVAILABLE

(PAGE INTENTIONALLY LEFT BLANK.)

CONTENT NOT AVAILABLE

☹

(PAGE INTENTIONALLY LEFT BLANK.)

CONTENT NOT AVAILABLE

☹

(PAGE INTENTIONALLY LEFT BLANK.)

CONTENT NOT AVAILABLE

(PAGE INTENTIONALLY LEFT BLANK.)

CHAPTER VI

OPEC IS OUR FRIEND... LET ME EXPLAIN

CONTENT NOT AVAILABLE

☹

(PAGE INTENTIONALLY LEFT BLANK.)

CONTENT NOT AVAILABLE

(PAGE INTENTIONALLY LEFT BLANK.)

CONTENT NOT AVAILABLE

(PAGE INTENTIONALLY LEFT BLANK.)

CONTENT NOT AVAILABLE

☹

(PAGE INTENTIONALLY LEFT BLANK.)

CONTENT NOT AVAILABLE

(PAGE INTENTIONALLY LEFT BLANK.)

CONTENT NOT AVAILABLE

☹

(PAGE INTENTIONALLY LEFT BLANK.)

CONTENT NOT AVAILABLE

☹

(PAGE INTENTIONALLY LEFT BLANK.)

CONTENT NOT AVAILABLE

(PAGE INTENTIONALLY LEFT BLANK.)

CONTENT NOT AVAILABLE

(PAGE INTENTIONALLY LEFT BLANK.)

CONTENT NOT AVAILABLE

(PAGE INTENTIONALLY LEFT BLANK.)

CONTENT NOT AVAILABLE

(PAGE INTENTIONALLY LEFT BLANK.)

CHAPTER VII

HOW ENVIRONMENTALISTS HELP OUR COUNTRY

CONTENT NOT AVAILABLE

(PAGE INTENTIONALLY LEFT BLANK.)

CONTENT NOT AVAILABLE

☹

(PAGE INTENTIONALLY LEFT BLANK.)

CONTENT NOT AVAILABLE

(PAGE INTENTIONALLY LEFT BLANK.)

CONTENT NOT AVAILABLE

☹

(PAGE INTENTIONALLY LEFT BLANK.)

CONTENT NOT AVAILABLE

☹

(PAGE INTENTIONALLY LEFT BLANK.)

CONTENT NOT AVAILABLE

(PAGE INTENTIONALLY LEFT BLANK.)

CONTENT NOT AVAILABLE

(PAGE INTENTIONALLY LEFT BLANK.)

CONTENT NOT AVAILABLE

☹

(PAGE INTENTIONALLY LEFT BLANK.)

CONTENT NOT AVAILABLE

(PAGE INTENTIONALLY LEFT BLANK.)

CONTENT NOT AVAILABLE

☹

(PAGE INTENTIONALLY LEFT BLANK.)

CONTENT NOT AVAILABLE

☹

(PAGE INTENTIONALLY LEFT BLANK.)

CHAPTER VIII

HOW CARBON CREDITS WILL GROW OUR ECONOMY

CONTENT NOT AVAILABLE

(PAGE INTENTIONALLY LEFT BLANK.)

CONTENT NOT AVAILABLE

☹

(PAGE INTENTIONALLY LEFT BLANK.)

CONTENT NOT AVAILABLE

☹

(PAGE INTENTIONALLY LEFT BLANK.)

CONTENT NOT AVAILABLE

(PAGE INTENTIONALLY LEFT BLANK.)

CONTENT NOT AVAILABLE

(PAGE INTENTIONALLY LEFT BLANK.)

CONTENT NOT AVAILABLE

☹

(PAGE INTENTIONALLY LEFT BLANK.)

CONTENT NOT AVAILABLE

(PAGE INTENTIONALLY LEFT BLANK.)

CONTENT NOT AVAILABLE

☹

(PAGE INTENTIONALLY LEFT BLANK.)

CONTENT NOT AVAILABLE

☹

(PAGE INTENTIONALLY LEFT BLANK.)

CONTENT NOT AVAILABLE

(PAGE INTENTIONALLY LEFT BLANK.)

CONTENT NOT AVAILABLE

(PAGE INTENTIONALLY LEFT BLANK.)

CHAPTER IX

MY CASE AGAINST DRILLING IN ANWR

CONTENT NOT AVAILABLE

☹

(PAGE INTENTIONALLY LEFT BLANK.)

CONTENT NOT AVAILABLE

☹

(PAGE INTENTIONALLY LEFT BLANK.)

CONTENT NOT AVAILABLE

(PAGE INTENTIONALLY LEFT BLANK.)

CONTENT NOT AVAILABLE

☹

(PAGE INTENTIONALLY LEFT BLANK.)

CONTENT NOT
AVAILABLE

(PAGE INTENTIONALLY LEFT BLANK.)

CONTENT NOT AVAILABLE

☹

(PAGE INTENTIONALLY LEFT BLANK.)

CONTENT NOT AVAILABLE

☹

(PAGE INTENTIONALLY LEFT BLANK.)

CONTENT NOT AVAILABLE

☹

(PAGE INTENTIONALLY LEFT BLANK.)

CONTENT NOT AVAILABLE

(PAGE INTENTIONALLY LEFT BLANK.)

CONTENT NOT AVAILABLE

☹

(PAGE INTENTIONALLY LEFT BLANK.)

CONTENT NOT AVAILABLE

(PAGE INTENTIONALLY LEFT BLANK.)

CONTENT NOT AVAILABLE

☹

(PAGE INTENTIONALLY LEFT BLANK.)

CONTENT NOT AVAILABLE

☹

(PAGE INTENTIONALLY LEFT BLANK.)

CHAPTER X

HOW THE AIRLINE INDUSTRY CAN GO ELECTRIC

CONTENT NOT AVAILABLE

(PAGE INTENTIONALLY LEFT BLANK.)

CONTENT NOT AVAILABLE

☹

(PAGE INTENTIONALLY LEFT BLANK.)

CONTENT NOT AVAILABLE

☹

(PAGE INTENTIONALLY LEFT BLANK.)

CONTENT NOT AVAILABLE

☹

(PAGE INTENTIONALLY LEFT BLANK.)

CONTENT NOT AVAILABLE

(PAGE INTENTIONALLY LEFT BLANK.)

CONTENT NOT AVAILABLE

(PAGE INTENTIONALLY LEFT BLANK.)

CONTENT NOT AVAILABLE

(PAGE INTENTIONALLY LEFT BLANK.)

CONTENT NOT AVAILABLE

☹

(PAGE INTENTIONALLY LEFT BLANK.)

CONTENT NOT AVAILABLE

☹

(PAGE INTENTIONALLY LEFT BLANK.)

CONTENT NOT AVAILABLE

(PAGE INTENTIONALLY LEFT BLANK.)

CONTENT NOT AVAILABLE

(PAGE INTENTIONALLY LEFT BLANK.)

CONTENT NOT AVAILABLE

☹

(PAGE INTENTIONALLY LEFT BLANK.)

CONTENT NOT AVAILABLE

(PAGE INTENTIONALLY LEFT BLANK.)

CONTENT NOT AVAILABLE

☹

(PAGE INTENTIONALLY LEFT BLANK.)

CONTENT NOT AVAILABLE

(PAGE INTENTIONALLY LEFT BLANK.)

CHAPTER XI

MY LETTER OF APPRECIATION TO THE OIL INDUSTRY

CONTENT NOT AVAILABLE

(PAGE INTENTIONALLY LEFT BLANK.)

CONTENT NOT AVAILABLE
☹

(PAGE INTENTIONALLY LEFT BLANK.)

CONTENT NOT AVAILABLE

☹

(PAGE INTENTIONALLY LEFT BLANK.)

CONTENT NOT AVAILABLE

☹

(PAGE INTENTIONALLY LEFT BLANK.)

CONTENT NOT AVAILABLE

(PAGE INTENTIONALLY LEFT BLANK.)

CONTENT NOT AVAILABLE

☹

(PAGE INTENTIONALLY LEFT BLANK.)

CONTENT NOT AVAILABLE

(PAGE INTENTIONALLY LEFT BLANK.)

CONTENT NOT AVAILABLE

☹

(PAGE INTENTIONALLY LEFT BLANK.)

CONTENT NOT AVAILABLE

☹

(PAGE INTENTIONALLY LEFT BLANK.)

CONTENT NOT AVAILABLE

☹

(PAGE INTENTIONALLY LEFT BLANK.)

CONTENT NOT AVAILABLE

(PAGE INTENTIONALLY LEFT BLANK.)

CONTENT NOT AVAILABLE

☹

(PAGE INTENTIONALLY LEFT BLANK.)

CONTENT NOT AVAILABLE

☹

(PAGE INTENTIONALLY LEFT BLANK.)

OBAMALOGUE

Obama's strategy for achieving energy independence in the U.S. will surely produce some great business opportunities when you consider the potential outcomes of his beliefs and policies.

But first, we have compiled a list of businesses to avoid in the future if Obama enacts his energy platform:

- **Oil & gas:** Obviously this sector produces too much pollution and greed.   Liquidate your holdings A.S.A.P.
- **Coal:** Refer to bullet point #1.
- **Automobiles:** What will you expect them to run on after gasoline is outlawed...lithium batteries? Where would you suggest we store 1 billion used batteries per year?
- **Wind energy:** Wind mills kill bird migrations. That's horrible.
- **Solar power:** Bad idea. If you care about the Desert Tortoise you will avoid this sector.
- **Nuclear:** N.I.M.B.Y.!! Need I say more?

Well, so much for the old way of doing things. Now let's take a look at the opportunities that will emerge as a result of Mr. Obama's grand vision:

- **The buggy whip:** Imagine 125 million cars no longer on our roads. What is the replacement option? Horse and buggy of course. If

I were you, I would invest in a buggy whip web site, or in horse breeding farms.

- **Fertilizer industry:** Think about how much fertilizer we will produce with several hundred million horses on our roads. OK it might smell a bit, but you know the routine...the unintended consequences of good intentions.
- **Shovels:** Refer to 'several hundred million horses on our roads.'
- **Bicycles:** China is finally converting from bikes to cars, while we will be converting from cars to bikes. Goodbye super power, hello 3rd world status.
- **Wax:** Since we won't be able to rely on gas, oil, coal, and nuclear for our power needs, the candle making industry will once again burn brightly.
- **Sailboat container ships:** Estimated delivery time...6 months.
- **Hand fans:** You might want to invest in this arena, especially if you live in the sun belt.

Please keep in mind, these businesses represent just a few of the opportunities that will avail themselves to us as a result of Obama's vision.

Now we know what Obama meant by the statement **'hope and change.'**

Those of you who voted for him should have asked for a definition.

Remember, 2012 is right around the corner, and our return to free market capitalism is waiting.

This book should be placed on every coffee table in America.

www.ingramcontent.com/pod-product-compliance
Lightning Source LLC
Chambersburg PA
CBHW060304290526
45789CB00001B/405